I0142312

365 Reminders of
The Importance of Living
Happy

Sally Huss

Copyright © 2020 Sally Huss/Huss Publishing
All rights reserved.
ISBN: 9781945742613

Words matter. Thoughts come first. We send our thoughts out into the world, accompanied by the feelings that go with them. Before reaching outside ourselves however, the thoughts we think and often share in words go through our own being first to either elevate us or not. Think good thoughts.

Here you will find 365 lovely thoughts to start your days. Take each one, a day at a time, and savor it. If you love its meaning, share it with others.

We all need a little something to touch our hearts daily. These are thoughts of encouragement, suggestions to follow, inspirational messages, truths revealed, and nourishment for living happy!

You are dearly loved by the life that surrounds you, and your presence and efforts to uplift yourself and others are greatly appreciated.

Don't forget: happy days are made by happy people. Happy people are made by choice!

Day 1
Kiss the day in the morning
and surely it will kiss you back by night.

Day 2
Every heart counts, especially yours.

Day 3
Silence contains more than words can say.

Day 4
To age is easy.
To age gracefully takes some effort.

Day 5
Love is all there is worth having
or giving or being.

Day 6
The days we keep are the days
we are thankful for.

Day 7
Life smiles on those who smile on it.

Day 8
The strides you take are not as important
as taking everything in stride.

Day 9
Life should be celebrated… continuously.

Day 10
Matters of the heart matter most.

Day 11
The unintended consequences of kindness
is more of the same.

Day 12
A significant other is anyone in your presence.

Day 13
Peace is an inside job.

Day 14
Life includes you in its every thought.

Day 15
A day filled with joy awaits your involvement.

Day 16
Kindness is good. Kindness is wise.
Kindness is necessary.

Day 17
A person who is like the sun,
shining equally on everyone, is very great indeed.

Day 18
Forget the mask. Forget the face. Forget the skin.
Love the within, love the heart.

Day 19
As you take care of today,
tomorrow takes care of itself.

Day 20
Rich is a matter of the heart.

Day 21
In the realm of help, hope reigns supreme.

Day 22
Fill a child with enough love to last a lifetime
and that child will grow up to do the same.

Day 23
Honor your past. Honor your future.
Honor yourself. Take a bow.

Day 24
Life sings only love songs. Listen carefully.

Day 25
Worry less or not at all.

Day 26
Focus on the positive and the rest
will fall away from lack of interest.

Day 27
Miracles tumble out of the sky
and fall into the laps of those who expect them.

Day 28
Along every path
beautiful experiences are gathered.

Day 29
Little thoughts of self-appreciation
make a big difference to oneself.

Day 30
Life is about sowing. Reaping is only that
you have more to sow with.

Day 31
Best wishes are sent to you daily
by the love that surrounds you always.

Day 32
Know that all is well always
and everything is unfolding as it should.

Day 33
Your future is bright when you shine on it.

Day 34
Fall in love with life.
Life is already in love with you.

Day 35
Make your goals crystal clear
and clearly they will become crystalized,
provided life doesn't have something better in mind.

Day 36
Happiness does not come uninvited.
It needs to be the guest of honor.

Day 37
To love the way it is, is wise.
To love the way it isn't, is just as wise.

Day 38
You can find something beautiful anywhere
you look, it you are looking for something beautiful.

Day 39
Fear lacks support from those who trust life.

Day 40
That which touches the heart touches everyone.
That which touches everyone is worth everything.

Day 41
Treated gently things become gentle, even people.

Day 42
Your work is something you do, not what you are.
What you are is far greater than anything you can do.

Day 43
Pleasantries do not go unnoticed.
Be as pleasant as possible.

Day 44
The unexpected is all that anyone can expect.

Day 45
One who is generous with praise
makes another rich in self-worth.

Day 46
Life works wonders on those
who think life is wonderful.

Day 47
Hope is eternal because change is inevitable.

Day 48
Timing is everything.
Whatever time it is, it's the right time.

Day 49
We sail through life as life sails through us.

Day 50
Do some good, then do some more.

Day 51
Some beauty is skin-deep.
Real beauty is heart-deep.

Day 52
Smile share. Everyone benefits.

Day 53
Kindness goes a long way to making a better world.

Day 54
A day without love is a day lost.

Day 55
To know, but not to judge; to love, but not to keep;
to be, but not to be asleep
is a way far better than most.

Day 56
Life is to be enjoyed.
Nature is to be worshipped.

Day 56
Give priority to that which makes you smile.

Day 57
Life is everything.
Guard it with everything you've got.

Day 58
Quiet beauty finds its way into the heart.

Day 59
Difficult people help us grow.
Be sure to thank them.

Day 60
Days ahead are days within
perfectly created by attending to the days now.

Day 61
Selfishly guard the heart's ability to love,
then generously share its contents.

Day 62
Of all the treasures in the world,
a friend is the greatest.

Day 63
Enjoy this day. It is only here for today
and will never come again.

Day 64
Relaxation is highly underestimated.
Ask a cat.

Day 65
Trust life. It will never let you down.

Day 66
Never break a heart, especially your own.

Day 67
Our gift is time.
Our gift in return is to use it wisely.

Day 68
Joyfully one enters the state of joy.

Day 69
Smiling is a habit not easily broken.

Day 70
Everyday occurrences might just be
ordinary miracles.

Day 71
The only thing better than the nearness of flowers
are the closeness of friends.

Day 72
Take every day as it comes. It comes perfectly.

Day 73
Heart-touches move us beyond ourselves.

Day 74
Life is not meant to be easy... wonderful yes,
but not easy.

Day 75
If you are not living life to the fullest, reach higher.

Day 76
Accomplishments are their own reward.
Be sure to enjoy them.

Day 77
Remember to forget all those unpleasant things
that are so easy to remember.

Day 78
Be pleased with what life serves you
and you will be pleasantly surprised by dessert.

Day 79
If you are blessed with work, be sure you know it.

Day 80
Every friend has a special place in one's heart.
Make lots of room.

Day 81
When change is needed,
a change of attitude is usually called for.

Day 82
A human being is a work in progress.
Be patient.

Day 83
On the highway of life, take the high road.

Day 84
Your worth is invaluable.
Your knowing it is priceless.

Day 85
You can only do what you do and be what you are.
Enjoy yourself!

Day 86
To be a friend is a kindness of great proportion.

Day 87
Settle down with harmony and live happily ever after.

Day 88
Greater than the thought of you, is you.

Day 87
Each part of a family adds to the heart of a family
and the heart of a family is love.

Day 88
Just when you think you're out of miracles,
life sends in a boatload full.

Day 89
The results take care of themselves
when you take care of everything else.

Day 90
The best equipment to have in life
is a set of open arms.

Day 91
Willpower is highly misunderstood. When used,
it works fine. When not, it does no good.

Day 92
Mistakes are welcome.
We can't learn without them.

Day 93
We are all in the same boat – life.
Keep paddling!

Day 94
Your attitude toward the gift of life
you have been given determines everything.

Day 95
The need for peace is greater than
the need for anxiety. Help out!

Day 96
Your time is your life. Be sure you are having
the time of your life with the life of your time.

Day 97
Ever full is the well of happiness. Use a big bucket!

Day 98
Great thoughts perpetuate themselves. Think big!

Day 99
When one blessing fades, another takes its place.

Day 100
The sun rises to every occasion.
You can do the same.

Day 101
Live happy! Life is better that way.

Day 102
What you accomplish outside is nothing
compared to what you can accomplish inside.

Day 103
Way beyond words is the heart.
Fortunately it's so close!

Day 104
We live busy lives. We live exciting lives.
But do we live meaningful lives?

Day 105
All times are good times. Difficult times
help us grow. Happy times remind us to enjoy.

Day 106
What life has in store for you is greater
than what you have in store for yourself.

Day 107
You are fully funded in you heart for what lies ahead.

Day 108
Of all that matters, love matters most.

Day 109
Even when kindness is used, it is never used up.

Day 110
A moment lost to sorrow cannot be retrieved,
no matter how sorry you are.

Day 111
When something is done with love,
it is done to perfection!

Day 112
To know that your life means more than
what it means to you, is well worth knowing.

Day 113
Helping hands are gladly shaken.

Day 114
Smiles sound the same in every language. Speak up!

Day 115
Big-hearted people show themselves
for what they are by what they do.

Day 116
The jewels in your life are the friends in your life.
Treasure them all.

Day 117
Talents are gifts to be used.
Be sure you are using yours.

Day 118
Thank goodness for you.
Without you the puzzle of life would be incomplete.

Day 119
Love is work assigned to everyone.

Day 120
Fill yourself to the brim with happiness
and you will be overjoyed with the results.

Day 121
Good-hearted people do us all good.

Day 122
Silence speaks of that which is truly important.

Day 123
One is never so tall as when one reaches down
to help a child.

Day 124
Goodness matters, for goodness sake!

Day 125
Forward thinking people have a lot
to look forward to.

Day 126
Whatever amount of your greatness that
you have showing, you've only scratched the surface.

Day 127
Life is about hurdles – high hurdles and low hurdles.
May you clear them all with the same glee.

Day 128
Give a person a goal and you will have given
that person a reason to be.

Day 129
Happiness is within and should be coaxed
from its hiding place whenever possible.

Day 130
What passes between people is a feeling.
More is not said than is said.

Day 131
It's not where you've been,
but where you're going that counts.

Day 132
At the heart of every person
is the heart of every other person.

Day 133
Assume the best. You're sure to be close!

Day 134
Don't take yourself personally.
We belong to each other.

Day 135
Doing good, feeling good, and speaking good
bring good luck.

Day 136
The game of life requires your participation –
enthusiastically!

Day 137
We are all in the service of each other.
Make it a labor of love.

Day 138
One feels wonderful when one is full of wonder.

Day 139
Anxiety relaxes its grip
when love takes hold of the heart.

Day 140
When a 'thank you' is close at hand,
there will be a lot to be thankful for.

Day 141
The more you love, the more you will love.

Day 142
If you can't take it with you, it's not worth keeping.

Day 143
Make trusted friends by starting with yourself.

Day 144
Special people come into your life
at just the right time. Who sends them?

Day 145
Keep your sunny side up,
whether you're an egg or not.

Day 146
Like apples, we all have cores.
It is where the seeds of contentment are stored.

Day 147
When your cup runneth over, share!

Day 148
You can count on miracles. You just can't count
on what they will be or when they will show up.

Day 149
Do not dismiss the day of small happenings.
Great things are always in the works.

Day 150
Kind words are easily spoken.

Day 151
To go from ordinary to extraordinary
takes just a little extra.

Day 152
Your thoughts are your future.
Make them glorious.

Day 153
A moment of bliss can last a lifetime,
if it is nourished and held tightly.

Day 154
People are as divine as they think they are.

Day 155
Humble pie tastes good to a grateful heart.

Day 156
Life beckons in the direction of good tirelessly.

Day 157
Great things are done by people
who know their own greatness.

Day 158
The need to express kindness is as great
as the need to receive kindness.

Day 159
Swallow a good thought and it can
flavor your whole day.

Day 160
Positive efforts yield positive results positively!

Day 161
In everything, the beginning is the most important.
Begin with a smile.

Day 162
Angels come in many disguises, even as friends.

Day 163
Stick with truth. It's a good life companion.

Day 164
In the garden of people, friends are the roses.

Day 165
Keep your chin up. It's where it's happiest.

Day 166
Wishful thinking gets you where you want to go.

Day 167
When things are easy, it is easy to be happy.
When things are tough, it is essential to be happy.

Day 168
Life is a gift. Act accordingly!

Day 169
The happier you are, the happier you get.

Day 170
An army of angels keeps in step
with a person who dances with life.

Day 171
Not a day goes by when a little kindness
doesn't make it better.

Day 172
It's the giving, not the keeping that makes us happy.

Day 173
Life passes over the passive ones,
waiting for them to come to life.

Day 174
If life were easy, we wouldn't grow.
If we didn't grow,
we wouldn't know how great life is.

Day 175
People are full of surprises. Thank goodness!

Day 176
A kind gesture is always welcome.

Day 177
Someone is looking out for you,
whether you know it or not.

Day 178
Joy lasts as long as you remember
that it belongs to you.

Day 179
Best wishes float in the air
waiting for you to breathe them in.

Day 180
Quietly we can know ourselves. Listen.

Day 181
Blessings cannot be counted often enough.

Day 182
Truth has a certain ring to it.
It sounds good to everyone.

Day 183
To love harmony makes it yours.

Day184
Picture a happy life and soon
you will be able to put a frame around it.

Day 185
Life polishes us – sometimes gently,
sometimes roughly, but always for the better.

Day 186
Wisdom watches over us,
hoping we'll steal a little from its treasure trove.

Day 187
There is opportunity behind every new door.

Day 188
A simple moment of peace
can make a big difference in a hectic life.

Day 189
A change of mind and a change of heart
must go hand in hand before a real change occurs.

Day 190
When thinking, the sky's the limit!

Day 191
Going with the flow seems too good to be true.

Day 192
If you need a sign that you are loved,
look at the sun.

Day 193
Make the space you walk through better
for your having been there. Your affect is enormous.

Day 194
Kindness is priceless.

Day 195
Life's merry-go-round goes round and round
and up and down. At every point it is still merry.

Day 196
Flowers like to show off.
Be sure to tell them how beautiful they are.

Day 197
Happy people are rich,
whether they have any money or not.

Day 198
To be a sun in the lives of others is a good thing.
Knowing where that sunshine comes from
is even better.

Day 199
Learning to love listening to the heart
is a skill of infinite value.

Day 200
Breathing deeply reminds us to live less shallowly.

Day 201
The only time you're past your prime
is when you think you are.

Day 202
The practice of loving kindness
sets in motion all kinds of blessings.

Day 203
Fearlessly go forward. Life is holding your hand.

Day 204
Now counts. Make the most of it!

Day 205
Life is better when it is taken as it comes.

Day 206
To find good times in hard times is an art
worth cultivating.

Day 207
A good thought is worth
a thousand words, but shorter.

Day 208
Love is a renewable source of energy.
Use it freely.

Day 209
Given a choice, pick harmony every time.

Day 210
Give for the fun of it.

Day 211
When you realize that everything is a gift,
life takes on a different meaning.

Day 212
Doing the right thing is more important
than being right.

Day 213
A loving person is never alone.

Day 214
Take pleasure in little things.
The big things come and go.

Day 215
Through the eyes of love,
everything is more beautiful.

Day 216
Good thoughts and good feelings
lead to good results. Guaranteed!

Day 217
In times of shortage,
there's plenty of room for kindness.

Day 218
Today is a good day to feel blessed.

Day 219
If you wait to be happy, you will wait forever.
If you are happy now, you will be happy forever.

Day 220
Life is a voyage in which we constantly trim our sails
for a better future.

Day 221
Follow your heart fearlessly
and you'll find yourself just where you want to be.

Day 222
Abundance is in the eyes of the beholder.

Day 223
On the wings of each other, we are uplifted.

Day 224
Beyond your wildest dreams are the things
you can accomplish by making a decision to do so.

Day 225
Your potential for greatness is greater than you think.

Day 226
If you can't find a reason to be happy,
make one up.

Day 227
In the face of sunlight, everything is bright.

Day 228
Just when you think you've got your ducks in a row,
life changes the line up. Stay flexible!

Day 229
Old people can be any age, just like young people.

Day 230
More than bliss, life cannot promise.

Day 231
The kindest gestures towards one
are felt by everyone.

Day 232
Life is wonderful. Don't forget it!

Day 233
We are all the way we are for a lot of reasons
and for all those reasons and more
we are worthy of being loved.

Day 234
Give yourself the stamp of approval.
You'll find no higher award.

Day 235
Dancing with the feet is one thing.
Dancing with the heart is another.

Day 236
The seeds of goodness always yield good crops.

Day 237
Every day offers a fresh start. How kind of life!

Day 238
A heart full of thankfulness is always content.

Day 239
Self-love, self-worth, and self-esteem
are the basic necessities of life.

Day 240
Listen up! Listen to that which is higher.

Day 241
The better you feel, the better the world seems.
The better the world seems, the better you feel.

Day 242
We all get our just desserts.
Some are sweeter than others.

Day 243
Life is a serious matter, best taken light-heartedly.

Day 244
Smiles never go out of style.
They are more popular now than ever.

Day 245
Blissfully approach the day.
You never know what bliss will bring.

Day 246
The heart asks few questions
because it has most answers.

Day 247
Only from a place of harmony
can we move forward.

Day 248
Everything worth giving and keeping is within.

Day 249
Stretch your greatness, then watch it soar.

Day 250
The sun shines continuously.
Even a few clouds can't dampen its spirit.

Day 251
Every good thought has a happy ending.

Day 252
To be wildly successful, you need to be
utterly fearless – and kind too.

Day 253
No matter where you want to go
here is where you start.

Day 254
A lucky day is one you awaken to.

Day 255
What goes around comes around.
Go around happy!

Day 256
Better than having things are having qualities.

Day 257
Rich is the state you find yourself in
when you're not worried about money.

Day 258
The only way to know your own greatness
is to try it out.

Day 259
Keep on keepin' on, then keep on some more.

Day 260
Relish the ground you walk on.
There's a tickle in each step.

Day 261
Be yourself! No one can do it better.

Day 262
Underneath the hubbub of daily life
is the harmony of nature. How reassuring.

Day 263
Pearls of wisdom may be worn anytime, anywhere.

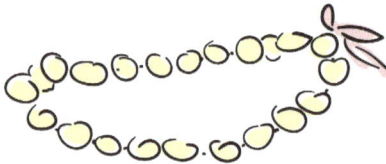

Day 264
Circumstances are neutral. It's the attitude
toward them that makes the difference.

Day 265
Kindness works wonders on every kind of hurt.

Day 266
Hope is the best of all life-extenders.

Day 267
If you are looking for an opportunity to be grateful,
one is sure to show up.

Day 268
Take heart. All roads lead to love.

Day 269
Wise is the one who loves himself unconditionally.

Day 270
Better than you, you cannot find.
Better than kind, you cannot be.

Day 271
Lean into what feels good
and away from what doesn't.

Day 272
The future is wide open. Go for it!

Day 273
Life is full of good reasons to trust it.

Day 274
Make efforts that make a difference.
They take just as much effort as those that don't.

Day 275
Anxiety has proven to be useless in all cases.

Day 276
Sunrise brings with it blessings of infinite number.

Day 277
Romance is more than a box of chocolates.
It holds the delicious possibility of love.

Day 278
Wise people keep their own counsel.

Day 279
Will wonders never cease? Never!

Day 280
Insight comes on the back of intuition.

Day 281
Keep your eye on your thoughts.
They're the stuff your future is made of.

Day 282
Rich is good. Wisdom is good.
Rich in wisdom is better.

Day 283
Stand firm on feeling good. It's where you stand best.

Day 284
Keep your longings a long way off.
Reaching for them will keep you inspired.

Day 285
It's nice to be needed. Everyone is.

Day 286
Cultivate happiness today
and it will spill over onto tomorrow.

Day 287
A perfectly formed day arrives every morning.

Day 288
Life loves to be appreciated. Who doesn't?

Day 289
Dancing puts a smile on your feet. Keep shuffling.

Day 290
When you're open for opportunities,
you're open for business.

Day 291
Wherever you find love,
you can be sure a happy heart is nearby.

Day 292
Joy is available regardless of circumstances.
Might as well use it.

Day 293
A smile can uplift another
as fast as it can uplift oneself.

Day 294
The best things in life are free
and they are becoming more popular than ever.

Day 295
Life is good and better because you are in it.

Day 296
The sun rains that which is truly important – light.

Day 297
The creation that exists is not our doing.
Our doing is to appreciate it.

Day 298
A good mood starts with a smile.

Day 299
You're never too old to act young.

Day 300
Attitude is everything. Pick a good one!

Day 301
You are as worthy as you think you are.

Day 302
Expect the best and the best will surely show up!

Day 303
Love binds ever so sweetly.

Day 304
Life is a mirror. Be sure to smile.

Day 305
Be a constant example of what it means
to be a friend.

Day 306
Work with love
and you'll feel like you're not working at all.

Day 307
The gift of life lasts a lifetime. Use it well.

Day 308
An authentic you is as good as you get.

Day 309
If you value what money can't buy,
your point of view is priceless!

Day 310
The effects of gratitude are greater than you think.

Day 311
Tender-hearted people help warm the world.

Day 312
Positive words tickle the heart
and brighten the day for anyone who hears them.

Day 314
Act with loving kindness
for the most favorable outcomes.

Day 315
Once you 'Will' to do 'Good,'
there is no end to the good you can do.

Day 316
Divine love solves all problems.

Day 317
Quiet times open the door for knowing. Shhhh!

Day 318
An eraser for the past. An empty page for the future.
A world of possibilities for the here and now.

Day 319
Look to give. Prepare to receive.

Day 320
Get happy. Be happy. Stay happy.
A happy future depends on it.

Day 321
Clarity is a necessity in times of confusion
and times that are not.

Day 322
If you see a worry coming, duck!

Day 323
The more you notice the good things in life,
the more good things show up.

Day 324
Life agrees most sincerely with what you think.
Think happy thoughts.

Day 325
If you live to love, you will love to live!

Day 326
If you've got breath, you've got life.
If you've got life, you've got everything.

Day 327
Appreciate yourself, no one can do it for you.

Day 328
The value of falling down is the opportunity
to learn how to get up.

Day 329
When our nature is in harmony with Nature,
we blossom.

Day 330
It's the sun that makes a day.
Be sure to thank it.

Day 331
Every minute of every day is precious.
Have you noticed?

Day 332
Share your joys, not your troubles.

Day 334
An example replaces a thousand words.

Day 335
Worry lasts as long as you feed it.

Day 336
Each day is a lifetime to be lived fully,
joyfully and without regret.

Day 337
Whenever you need a kind word, speak up!

Day 338
Feathers in your cap come from talents well used.

Day 339
Live this day well. That's all you need to do.

Day 340
The accumulation of wealth
looks a lot like a gathering of friends.

Day 341
Breathe in whatever you truly need.
The air is full of it.

Day 342
Lighten up! Life loves a happy camper.

Day 343
Your enthusiasm for life will see you through
any obstacle that life throws your way.

Day 344
The value you give a day is invaluable to you.

Day 345
When you set an intention, set it in stone.

Day 346
If you like challenges, you will love life!

Day 347
Guide your will down the path of usefulness
and you will be delighted with where it takes you.

Day 348
Be pleased with 'Now.' It will be with you forever.

Day 349
Hold yourself in high esteem
and others will do the same.

Day 350
Moments of inspiration should be cherished.

Day 351
Keep all doors of opportunity open.
You don't know who
or what will come through them.

Day 352
Life keeps track of how you use your energies.
Use them well.

Day 353
The higher your ideal,
the more inclined you will be to work towards it.

Day 354
Grateful is as grateful does.

Day 355
Giving is true giving when nothing is asked in return.

Day 356
Effort is everything in accomplishing.

Day 357
Goodwill should be common practice.

Day 358
Eat for health. Play for fun. Work for joy.
Love for life.

Day 359
Character counts. You can count on it
and so can everyone else.

Day 360
When you enter the day thankfully,
all manner of good things follow.

Day 361
Believe in yourself.
You have everything you need at every moment.

Day 362
A compassionate heart is invaluable.
Put it to good use.

Day 363
Life is a bloomin' business.
Plant what you want to grow.

Day 364
Get ready; the best is yet to come!

Day 365
Dream big, plan well, work hard,
smile always, and good things will happen.

*****

Happy days are made by happy people. Happy people are made by choice.

Sally's prints are available on her website: sallyhuss.com

Author/Illustrator

Sally Huss

Author/illustrator Sally Huss creates books — and especially children's books. Her books uplift the lives of young children by giving them tools to overcome obstacles; by helping them value themselves and others; and by inspiring them to be the best that they can be. Her catalog of books now exceeds 100.

"Bright and happy," "light and whimsical" have been the catch phrases attached to the writings and art of Sally Huss for over 30 years. Sweet images dance across all of Sally's creations, whether in the form of children's books, paintings, wallpaper, ceramics, baby bibs, purses, clothing, or her King Features syndicated newspaper panel "Happy Musings."

Sally is a graduate of USC with a degree in Fine Art and through the years has had 26 of her own licensed art galleries throughout the world.

Here are a few more books by Sally that you might enjoy. All may be found on Amazon or on Sally's website – sallyhuss.com.

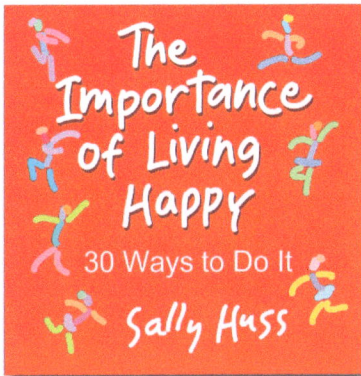

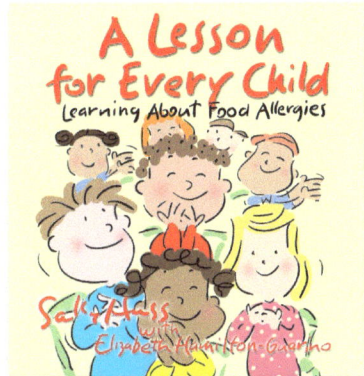

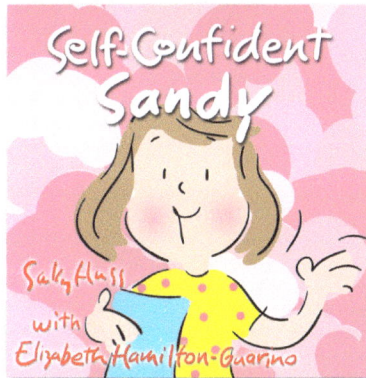

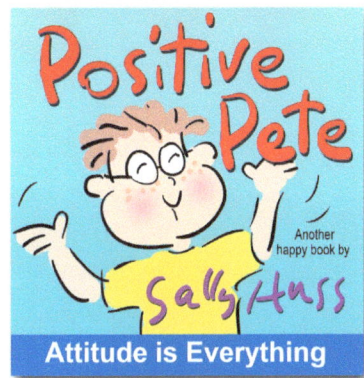

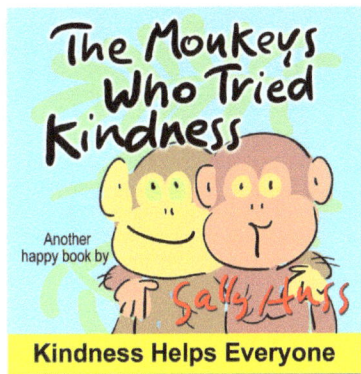

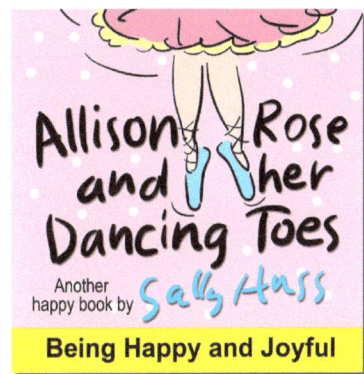

The Importance of Living Happy
30 Ways to Do It
Sally Huss

A Lesson for Every Child
Learning About Food Allergies
Sally Huss with Elizabeth Hamilton-Guarino

Self-Confident Sandy
Sally Huss with Elizabeth Hamilton-Guarino

Positive Pete
Another happy book by Sally Huss
Attitude is Everything

The Monkeys Who Tried Kindness
Another happy book by Sally Huss
Kindness Helps Everyone

Allison Rose and her Dancing Toes
Another happy book by Sally Huss
Being Happy and Joyful

www.ingramcontent.com/pod-product-compliance
Lightning Source LLC
LaVergne TN
LVHW010022070426
835508LV00001B/4